C000114781

Christ~~ian Fasting~~

Disciplining the body,
awakening the spirit

by
Sr Mary David Totah OSB

*All booklets are published thanks to the
generous support of the members of the
Catholic Truth Society*

CATHOLIC TRUTH SOCIETY
PUBLISHERS TO THE HOLY SEE

Contents

The nature of fasting

God has given us the goods of the earth, not only that we may enjoy them, but also that we may have the means of ... showing him our love by the voluntary renunciation of his gifts, and by the oblation of them to his glory. To abandon, for God's sake, all worldly enjoyments, has always been the practice of holy souls.

(*Saint Alphonsus de Liguori*)

A neglected spiritual practice

Fasting, in our days, has become one of the most neglected spiritual practices. Because of misunderstandings regarding the nature of fasting, Christians tend to fast very little, or disregard fasting altogether. Yet fasting was practised by Christ himself. After prayer and fasting for forty days in the wilderness, he victoriously faced the temptations of the devil (*Mt* 4:1-11). The Lord asked his disciples to use fasting as an important spiritual weapon to achieve spiritual victories (*Mt* 17:21; *Mk* 9:29; *Lk* 2:37). The example of the Lord was followed by his disciples (*Ac* 14:23; 27:9; 1 *Co* 7:5; 2

Co 11:27, etc.), and St Paul expressly speaks of fasting as a means by which Christians are to commend themselves as servants of God (2 *Co* 6:5).

Physical and spiritual aspects

In the Church's tradition, fasting is much more than a penance. Fasting for the Christian has two aspects: physical and spiritual, outward and inward. On the outward level, fasting involves physical abstinence from food and drink; yet rules about eating and drinking must never be treated as an end in themselves, for fasting has always an inward, spiritual purpose. Man is a unity of body and soul, and our fasting is a practice that involves both. So fasting will also include abstinence from evil thoughts, desires, and deeds.

Fasting to acquire purity of heart

Fasting is part of the struggle against weaknesses and defects to acquire purity of heart. It fosters prayer. It is a way of preparing the body for the resurrection, opening it to grace, and making it more receptive to God's word. Renouncing taste for earthly nourishment develops the taste for God. It is to liberate oneself from dependence on the things of this world in order to concentrate on the things of the Kingdom of God. According to St Seraphim, fasting is an "indispensable means" of gaining the fruit of the Holy Spirit in one's life, and Jesus himself taught that some forms of evil cannot be conquered without it. When the Apostles failed to heal a sick and suffering child, Christ explained that, "This kind (meaning the devil) can come out only by prayer and fasting" (*Mt* 17:21, *Mk* 9:29).[1] As St John Chrysostom comments: "These are like two wings that carry a person to the heights of God."

Fasting as a sign of expectation

But there is more. Fasting reminds us that Christians belong to a religious tradition which begins with a fall, connected with breaking a fast in Paradise, when Adam ate the forbidden fruit, and ends with the hope of a never-ending banquet. In between there is our Lord and his forty days of fasting, and the gift of his body and blood, in the form of the bread and wine from which we receive our daily nourishment. In such a framework eating and fasting are by no means negligible values. We fast in order to acknowledge the Lord as the true giver of good gifts; as the true Gift, the true Bread of Life, and as the One calling us to the banquet of his Kingdom. Fasting is ultimately for the sake of feasting. Abstaining through the forty days of Lent only makes sense if we are preparing to "be alleluia" throughout the fifty days of Easter. Fasting from the food and drink of this present world is for Christians a sign of expectation: we *expect to feast* on the food and drink of everlasting life in the new world, the world of the resurrection. So our fasting orients us towards Christ's second coming, just as the Eucharistic fast orients us towards receiving him at Mass.

We fast to purify eating and drinking

We do not fast because there is anything in itself unclean about the act of eating and drinking. Food and drink are, on the contrary, God's gift. Christians fast, not because they despise the divine gift, but to make themselves aware that it is indeed a gift. We fast to purify our eating and drinking, and to make them no longer a concession to greed but as sacrament, a means of communion with the Giver. So there is no question here of saying that fasting is a good thing because food and drink are bad things. That would be a kind of Gnosticism, a disparaging of God's creation. Food is not bad in itself; it is neither pure nor impure. As our Lord says, only what comes from the heart of man deserves such designations. St Thomas Aquinas says that if we have that negative attitude to food, our fasting is without Christian value. For him, fasting is part of the virtue of temperance, or self-control, which deals with acting rightly in areas of food, drink, and sexuality.

Temperance restrains the passions, ordering us towards our true good in this life and the next. And in all this he stresses that the worst vice is to lack proper esteem for the goodness of the world God has made, to fail take delight in the world God has made for our good.

Fasting is part of the natural law

It is said that St Gertrude rejoiced when better food appeared on the table on feast days, as children are happy when their parents have a party for them. Once when she was given a bunch of grapes, she heartily enjoyed the gift God had sent her, and that night Christ appeared to her with grapes in his hand to show his approval. So fasting out of disdain for food is not a good work. On the contrary, it is heresy. Nevertheless, for St Thomas, fasting is part of the natural law; it is found in all religious traditions. In fact if we do not fast we fail in our common humanity. This booklet is intended to explain the apparent paradox.

Fasting in other traditions

What the eyes are for the outer world, fasts are for the inner. (*Gandhi*)

Fasting or abstinence from food is not an exclusively Christian practice. It existed and still exists in other religious traditions, and even outside them, for example in some therapies or medical treatments. Fasts vary in their duration, motives, and modalities. There are occasional fasts, or regular fasts inscribed in a sacred calendar; the fast may be religious or simply natural, ascetic, medicinal, or political. In primitive religions, fasting was often practised before the hunt, or harvest, or before initiation ceremonies or other rituals, or to approach a deity or receive visions, as among certain American Indian tribes or among the Tugues of Siberia. Priestly groups among the Pueblo Indians fast during retreats before major ceremonies connected with changes in the seasons. Such forms of asceticism were believed to aid the faithful in their struggle against evil.

Sacred times

Fasting for special purposes or before or during sacred times is also characteristic of the major religions of the world. Buddhists fast on certain lunar days. In China, before the sacrifice during the night of the winter solstice when the heavenly Yang principle was believed to begin its new cycle, a fixed period of fasting and abstinence was observed. In India, Hindu *sadhus* or holy men are admired for their frequent personal fasts. Muslims fast for the thirty days of Ramadan, when they eat and drink nothing before sunset.

Social and political purposes

Fasting has also served certain social and political purposes. Mahatma Gandhi in the early part of the twentieth century used fasting as an effective strategy for his Satyagraha or Protest for the Truth campaign in India. He often called for collective fasts of twenty-four hours, on a national or local scale, for the sake of purification or penance. He conducted a fast in prison to atone for the excesses of his followers who would not practise his teaching of non-violence against British rule. He initiated a fast to death in 1934 in protest against untouchability and again in 1947 to stop bloodshed between Hindus and Muslims in Bengal and Delhi. But fasting for Gandhi always retained its religious, penitential significance: "A complete fast", he wrote, "is a complete and literal denial of self. It is the truest prayer."

Following Gandhi, fasting has frequently been practised to protest against war and social evils and injustices, as in the case of the black former comedian Dick Gregory in the US, who from the 1960s fasted on only water and fruit juice in protest against the violation of civil rights of American Indians and against US military activity in Southeast Asia. Similarly, the hunger prevailing in a great part of the globe has drawn many Christians to deprive themselves of one meal a week, the cost of which is given to charity. In this case, fasting is not only a form of public protest but also an awakening of consciousness and a form of solidarity.

Promoting the struggle for purity

Whether undertaken for religious, political, or ethical reasons, fasting and abstinence has been seen, even in non-Christian contexts, to promote a higher good and to sustain the struggle for purity. For both the religious person and the non-violent protester, fasting witnesses to the intensity of the desire, the seriousness of the concern, and the determination of the will to overcome evil.

Fasting in the Old Testament

The Mosaic Law (the divine law Moses received from God, as recorded in the first books of the Bible) prescribes one day of fasting, the Day of Atonement (Yom Kippur), the tenth day of the seventh month, which is usually September in our modern calendar (see *Nb* 29:7; *Lv* 16:29-31; 23:27-30). It consisted simply in eating nothing until evening for one day.

Turning towards God

In addition to this fast of the Jewish liturgy, the Old Testament gives examples of fasting undertaken before a difficult task (*Est* 4:16; *Jg* 20, 26), to implore pardon for a fault (1 *K* 21:27-29; *Jon* 3:5-7; cf. 1 *K* 21:9, 12; *Jl* 1:14 and 2:15), to mourn personal sorrow, as when King David fasted during the seven-day sickness of his infant son (2 *S* 12:16-22), to mark a national calamity (*Ba* 1:5; *Zc* 8:19), or on the eve of a battle or after a defeat (1 *S* 7:6; 1 *M* 3:47; *Jg* 20:26; 2 *S* 1:12). Esther's decisive intervention with the king to save her nation was preceded by three days of continual fasting, observed not only by the queen but also, at her orders, by all the Jews in the capital (*Est* 4:16). Judith's fast accompanied her widowhood, lasting three years and four months (*Jdt* 8:6). All the vicissitudes of life call for prayer reinforced by fasting. Fasting "humbles the soul" (*Lv* 16:29), offering proofs of distress and devotion to touch the heart of God. It is a form of prayer which hopes for everything from God (*Is* 58:3; *Jr* 14:2). For the prophets, fasting is an expression of a complete and radical turning of man towards God and his commandments, especially love of neighbour (*Is* 58:3; *Zc* 7:3; *Si* 34:30).

Fasting as a sign of repentance

This fast, accompanied by prayer, can be done by an individual or a community. In the second case, a decree is issued, "a fast is proclaimed", that obliges each member to observe it (1 *K* 21:9, 12; 2 *Ch* 20:3; *Is* 58:5; *Jr* 36:9; *Jl* 1:14, and 2:15). Ezra, in preparation for the journey from exile back to the Promised Land, called upon the assembled people to fast so that "we might humble ourselves before our God" (*Ez* 8:21). Although the duration is not mentioned, one can assume it is "until evening", suggesting that it was a single day's fast. God heard their prayer and assured them of his favour and protection. The people of Nineveh, responding to

Jonah's call to repentance, proclaimed a fast as a sign of their sincerity, saying: "Who knows, God may yet repent and turn from his fierce anger, so that we perish not?" (*Jon* 3:9). God saw their works and spared them.

After the exile there appear more commemorative fasts in the yearly calendar, like Yom Kippur, to mark the two terrible years of the fall of Jerusalem. In the fourth month of the breach of the walls of Jerusalem in 587 is commemorated; in the fifth month the capture of the city; in the seventh the assassination of Gedeliah; in the tenth the beginning of the siege (*Zc* 7:5 and 8:19).

Establishing humility

Fasting also appears in the Old Testament as a way of establishing oneself in humility, to place oneself in he presence of God or to receive a revelation. Thus both Moses (*Ex* 34:28) and Elijah (1 *K* 19:8) fast as a prelude to a meeting with God. Even though Daniel's fasts were accompanied by lamentations, they also precede revelations and express his desire to receive divine light (*Dn* 9:3; 10:12).

Personal devotion

It is clear, too, from references in the New Testament that pious Jews fasted out of personal devotion: "Night and day Anna served the Lord in fasts and prayers" (*Lk* 2:37). There is also the example of disciples of John the Baptist and the Pharisees (*Mk* 2:18), some of whom fasted twice a week (*Lk* 18:12).

Fasting in the teaching and mystery of Christ

Fasting was the commandment that was given to our nature in the beginning to protect it with respect to the tasting of food, and in this point the progenitor of our substance fell [Adam]...And the Saviour, also, when He manifested Himself to the world in the Jordan began at this point. For after His baptism the Spirit led him into the wilderness and He fasted forty days and forty nights. Likewise all who set out to follow in His footsteps make the beginning of the struggle upon this foundation. For this is a weapon forged by God, and who shall escape blame if he neglects it? And if the Lawgiver Himself fasts, who among those who keep the law has no need of fasting?

(*St Isaac the Syrian, Homilies*, 37)

Fasting in the Gospel

At first sight, it might seem that the early Christian practice of fasting could not be based on Christ's word and example. To be sure, Christ fasted for forty days and forty nights in the desert (*Mk* 4:2 and parallel passages), but to many of His contemporaries, He appeared to be "a glutton and a drunkard" (*Mt* 11:19) because He did not hesitate to eat with "tax collectors and sinners." He was asked why the disciples of the Pharisees and the disciples of John "fast often and offer prayers," while His disciples did not (*Lk* 5, 33). Did St Paul and the early Church in fact misunderstand Christ? By no means, for Christ did not reject fasting any more than He rejected prayer or almsgiving. In all these religious practices, He warned his disciples against every sort of hypocrisy and self-display:

> And when you fast, do not look dismal, like the hypocrites, for they disfigure their faces that their fasting may be seen by men. Truly I say to you, they have received their reward. But when you fast, anoint your head and wash your face that your fasting may not be seen by men but by your Father who is in secret; and you Father who sees in secret will reward you. (*Mt* 6:16-18)

So the disciples are to fast, but they are to do it solely for God's sake, not in order to be seen and praised. The same goes for prayer and almsgiving, and ultimately for the practice of all the virtues.

Moreover, Christ had a deeper reason for exempting his disciples at that time from customary fasts: *the presence of the Bridegroom* (*Mt* 9:15). Mentioned in all three Synoptic Gospels, this word of Jesus puts fasting in explicit relation to himself. The interruption of the fast is a sign of Christ's presence; fasting is connected with his absence. Thus it is a law of the church that no one fasts on the days when we especially celebrate Christ risen and newly present among us, whether it be the weekly Sunday or the fifty days of Paschaltide. That is why, too, the early monks broke their fast in the presence of guests in whom they saw the person of Christ.

The Fast and temptation of Christ

Matthew, Mark and Luke all recount how the Holy Spirit, immediately after coming upon Jesus at His baptism and consecrating Him as the anointed one, drove Him into the desert where He fasted for forty days and was put to the test by the devil. Christ thus inaugurated his ministry by a fast of forty days in an act of confident surrender to the Father.

The temptation of Our Lord occurs in three stages. First He is tempted to turn stones into bread; then to cast Himself down from the pinnacle of the temple in the expectation that God will help Him; and finally to prostrate before the devil in worship. In each instance Jesus cites a Scriptural text to repulse the devil's suggestion: "Man shall not live by bread alone" (*Dt* 8:3); "You shall not tempt the Lord your God" (*Dt* 6:16); "You shall worship the Lord your God and Him only shall you serve" (*Dt* 6:13) All three refer to the testing of Israel in the wilderness, after the crossing of the Red Sea. The three temptations then are a recapitulation of Israel's three trials in the desert; they are a summary of the history of Israel's path through the wilderness.[2]

The Israelites put God's patience, goodness, and power to the test. By their grumbling and defiance they challenge God. Jesus on the other hand keeps intact his Sonship through obedience to the word of God; He makes a great profession of faith which irradiates His whole existence. "Man shall not live by bread alone, but by every word that proceeds from the mouth of God" (*Mt* 4, 4). As Pope Benedict comments, "The true fast is thus directed to eating the 'true food,' which is to do the Father's will (cf. *Jn* 4, 34). If, therefore, Adam disobeyed the Lord's command 'of the tree of the knowledge of good and evil you shall not eat,' the believer, through fasting, intends to submit himself humbly to God, trusting in His goodness and mercy."

Jesus fasting shows utter dependence on God

Jesus' fasting is an external expression of His inner attitude of utter dependence on God. By refusing earthly nourishment, He showed His desire to be nourished by the Father's will. The three temptations are but one: the question of obedience and fidelity to God. The three Scriptural quotations are an intensification of one and the same thing: to live from the word of, not to put God to the test, to adore and serve him alone.

Paradise regained

Moreover, as noted by the Fathers of the Church, it is possible to see in this scene a recapitulation of the temptation of Adam and Eve in Paradise. In the commandment given by God to Adam to test his freedom and trust, the Fathers saw the commandment of fasting. Adam broke the fast by eating the forbidden fruit.

> "Just as Adam was driven out of paradise for having eaten, refusing to trust, so it is by fasting and faith that they who wish to enter paradise do so" (*Athanasius*).

"Fasting was established in paradise by law. For Adam received the first commandment: from the tree of the knowledge of good and evil you must not eat. But 'you must not eat' means fasting, and the beginning of the law. If Eve had fasted from the tree, we should not need this fast. For it is not the healthy who need a physician but they who are sick (*Mt* 9:12). We have become ill through sin; we are healed by penance. But penance without fasting is vain. The accursed earth shall bring forth thistles and thorns for thee. . .Because we did not fast we fell from paradise. Let us fast therefore that we may return to it" (*Basil the Great*).[3]

In his letter to St Eustochium of 384, St Jerome maintains that the first man was cast out of paradise because he obeyed his stomach instead of God, and that Satan even dared to tempt the Lord with hunger in the desert. Jerome says that fasting is to be practised so that we who have been cast out of paradise by the greed of Adam may regain it. One of the responsories in the Divine Office during Lent says: *Paradisi portas aperuit nobis ieunii tempus.* (*The doors of paradise have been opened to us by this time of fasting*).

The New Adam

So Adam broke the fast by eating the forbidden fruit. Christ the new Adam begins His redemptive work by fasting and restores man to paradise, to true life. He fasted not only to give His disciples an example, to teach them the great ascetical value of fasting in the fight against the temptation of the devil, Christ also fasted in the desert to triumph over the harmful effects of Adam's greed. According to St Ambrose, Christ's fasting did not only offer the faithful the example (*exemplum*) of how to guard against the treachery of the devil. In the perspective of salvation history (*mysterium*), it had first and foremost the effect of atoning for Adam's sin. Thanks to Christ's' fasting, the grace which the human race lost as a result of Adam's desire for the forbidden fruit is restored. From this perspective, fasting is no mere custom or obligation; it is connected with the very mystery of salvation.

Hunger is a spiritual state

Fasting is our participation in this experience of Christ by which He showed us that our dependency on food is not the whole truth about man, that hunger itself is also a spiritual state, and that it is in reality hunger for God. Christ comes to teach us to desire that nourishment which consists in accomplishing the will of God. Fasting reminds us that man does not live by bread alone but by every word that comes from the mouth of God. Fasting helps us to hunger for God. It is a privation, then, which opens us to the nourishment of the word.

The fast of the Church

The major fasts have been ordained by the holy apostles through the direction of the Holy Spirit, so that we too, in the common veneration of the Cross of Christ, should take some part in what He did for us.

(Pope St Leo the Great)

In spite of the paschal joy that suffused the early Church after Pentecost, the apostolic Church preserved the custom of fasting. In the Acts of the Apostles fasting and prayer preceded assignments to missionary work, a departure for the missions, a separation, as when the disciples in Antioch fast before allowing Saul and Barnabas to depart (*Ac* 13:2ff and 14:22). During his apostolic labours, Paul was not content to suffer hunger and thirst only when circumstances forced them on him. He added repeated fasts (2 *Co* 6:5; 11, 27; 1 *Co* 9:15-27).

The Didache

In a small work dating from the apostolic age *The teaching of the Lord to the Gentiles, through the twelve Apostles* (known nowadays as the *Didache*, i.e. the Teaching), fasting is prescribed for one or two days before baptism. This pre-baptismal fast refers to Our Lord's words: "This kind [of devil] can only come out through prayer and fasting" (*Mt* 17:21).

The *Didache* also prescribes fasting twice a week as in Judaism. Instead of fasting on Monday and Thursday as do the Jews, Christian will fast on Wednesdays and Fridays. This is the first mention of a practice that will structure the week for the entire ancient Church. In parable of the Publican and the Pharisee in Luke's gospel, the Pharisee congratulates himself on fasting twice a week. The two fast days are not specified by Luke, but the Didache tells us that they were Monday and Thursday. The Christian have therefore made this Jewish practice their own, while modifying it. The two days substituted for those of Judaism are chosen for their relation to Christ's passion, Wednesday being the day of His betrayal by Judas, Friday that of His passion and death. The first Christians thus realized the Lord's prediction: "The days will come when the Bridegroom is taken away from them, and then they will fast in those days (*Lk* 5:35).

Lent

In addition to this habit of fasting twice a week Church soon added other practices. Lent originated in the complete fast of one or two days preceding the feast of Easter. Even when the Lenten fast of forty days was later imposed on the whole Church, the Paschal fast proper, that is the whole of Holy Saturday until the vigil service, retained its strict obligatory character. When Pope St Gregory the Great, in the sixth century, was too ill to observe it one year, he felt unspeakable shame at the thought that even small children would be fasting on that day (*Dialogues* III, 33, 7). This period was extended first to one week, then to three and ended by comprising forty days, to commemorate Christ's forty days in the desert. St John Cassian describes Lent as "the tithes of the year," because it is roughly a tenth of the days in a year. In Lent we are giving these days to the Lord as a special offering, and in doing so, imitate his own fast as he intended us to do. And since baptism was administered during the night of the Paschal Vigil, this fast in preparation for Easter served also as a pre-baptismal fast. The Didache already prescribed fasting for one or two days before baptism; now all the faithful were invited to associate themselves, as far as they could, with the preparatory fast of their future brothers and sisters.

Vigils and Ember days

When new feasts were added to the liturgical calendar, the more important ones were given days of anticipation, called vigils. The fasts observed on those days imitated the Paschal fast. The fast of the *Ember Days*, which St Leo attributed to the Apostles, was in reality a later institution, incorporating, however, a very ancient element: this was the fast of Wednesday and Friday, to which a specifically Roman custom added Saturday. These were called "stations". The aim of these celebrations, which occurred every three months, was to solemnize the four seasons of the year. Also behind this practice was the memory of the Biblical fasts of the fourth, seven and tenth months. These four Ember weeks were meant to recall the ancient and venerable "stations" of each week in a Christian world which had abandoned the practice.

Rogation days

The fasts of the *Ember* seasons, like the twice-weekly fasts, were accompanied by common prayer, according to the Biblical tradition of prayer and fasting summed up in the words of Jesus. *Rogation days* were originally simply days of prolonged prayer. When people interrupted the prayer to eat, it was found that the meal lowered the spiritual temperature. It was a 5th century bishop of Vienne in Gaul, St Mamertus who remedied this by suppressing the dinner! The rogation prayers, combined with fasting, assumed a greater dignity and efficacy. Although Bishop Sidonius Apollinaris was little given to personal asceticism, he congratulated the bishop of Vienne and introduced into his own church of Clermont these liturgies of supplication strengthened by fasting.

In what did this fasting consist? Following the custom of the Jews, Christians first practised fasting by abstaining from all food until after sunset or after the recitation of Vespers, when the single meal of the day would be taken. In about the 9th century it became customary in some places to take the day's meal after the recitation of None, or about 3 p.m. Now it had been the custom on a fast day to say Mass only after the hour of None. To make allowance for the new custom of fasting, the hours of None and Vespers were anticipated and this led to the celebration of Mass earlier in the day. In the 12th century the custom of breaking one's fast at the hour of None everywhere prevailed, and by the 13th century the practice of taking the meal as early as noon became common.

A very light meal or collation is introduced

As the time of the single fast-day meal became earlier and earlier, a very light meal or collation became common at the end of the day. In the monasteries, where the days of fasting were much more numerous, the monks had much earlier distinguished between days of fast prescribed by the monastic rule and those observed by the Church. On the days of monastic—but not Church—fasts, the monks were allowed to take a drink in very moderate quantity or *collation* to be taken in the evening. Monastic practice thus provided the model for what became a general custom throughout the Church. By the 13th century taking something to drink apart from the day's meal was a generally accepted practice, and by the end of the 14th century it was common to take a collation of bread, vegetables or fruit. This collation, however, was never understood to be of a sufficient quantity to constitute a normal meal. In the 16th century a very light breakfast was approved. It was understood that at the collation not more than 8 ounces of solid food were to be eaten, and at breakfast, not more than 2 ounces.

Fasting as abstinence

But fasting was not only a question of quantity of food and times when it could be eaten. It also included abstinence from certain types of food, particularly flesh meat and meat products, including milk, eggs, butter and cheese. The original reason for our custom of eating pancakes on Shrove Tuesday was to use up any remaining eggs and butter before the Lenten fast began. Days of fasting were thus always days of abstinence from meat and meat products, although other non-fast days might be indicated for the observance of abstinence alone. The laws regarding abstinence, like those of fasting, were of unwritten origin and were subject to variations in custom in time and place.

General law until 1917

Until 1917 the general law of the Western Church required the faithful to fast on all the days of Lent except Sunday; on Wednesdays, Fridays and Saturdays of the Ember weeks; and on the vigils of Christmas, Pentecost, Assumption and All saints. By custom in many places, the Wednesdays and Fridays of Advent were also fast days. By fasting was understood the taking of only one main meal a day with abstinence from meat, eggs and milk products. Abstinence without fast was observed on all Fridays and Saturdays throughout the year. Local dispensations often mitigated these general prohibitions. Those engaged in hard labour, the very poor who had difficulty obtaining sufficient food at any time, and those in weak health or over fifty-nine years of age were excused from the law of fasting.

Privileges and dispensations

In 1917, Benedict XV granted the privilege of transferring a day of abstinence from the Saturdays of Lent to any other day of the week except Ash Wednesday and the Fridays of Lent. In 1941, Pius XII granted to all the bishops of the world the power to dispense entirely from fast and abstinence except on Ash Wednesday and Good Friday. Some restrictions on this faculty were imposed by the Holy See in 1949- namely that abstinence must be observed on all Fridays of the year; and fast and abstinence must be observed on Ash Wednesday, Good Friday and the vigils of the Assumption and Christmas. On days of fast and abstinence, eggs and milk products could be taken at breakfast and at the collation. In 1959, John XXIII granted to all the faithful permission to move the Christmas Eve fast and abstinence from the 24th to the 23rd of December.

A reorganization of discipline

Finally in the apostolic constitution *Poenitemini* of Pope Paul VI (17 February 1966) there was a reorganization of ecclesiastical discipline with regard to fasting and abstinence.

True penitence, however, cannot ever prescind from physical asceticism as well. Our whole being in fact, body and soul, (indeed the whole of nature, even animals without reason, as Holy Scripture often points out) must participate actively in this religious act whereby the creature recognizes divine holiness and majesty. The necessity of the mortification of the flesh also stands clearly revealed if we consider the fragility of our nature, in which, since Adam's sin, flesh and spirit have contrasting desires. This exercise of bodily mortification-far removed from any form of stoicism does not imply a condemnation of the flesh which sons of God deign to assume. On the contrary, mortification aims at the "liberation" of man, who often finds himself, because of concupiscence, almost chained by his own senses. Through "corporal fasting" man regains strength and the "wound inflicted on the dignity of our nature by intemperance is cured by the medicine of a salutary abstinence."

All Fridays and also Ash Wednesday were declared days of penitence. Abstinence is to be observed on every Friday that does not fall on a holy day of obligation, and fasting as well as abstinence on Ash Wednesday and Good Friday. It stated that the law of abstinence is to be understood as forbidding the use of meat, but not of eggs or milk products; and that the law of fasting permits only one full meal a day, but does not prohibit the taking of some food in the morning and in the evening provided that the requirements of local custom with regard to the quantity and quality of this supplementary nourishment are observed. The Constitution changed existing legislation with respect to that age at which is obliged by the law of abstinence from the completion of the 7th to the completion of the 14th year, and changed the age at which one ceases to be obliged by the laws of fasting to one's 60th year.

A more perfect form of fasting

The conciliar decree *Christus Dominus* on the pastoral office of bishops declared that it was the task of Episcopal conferences to transfer for just cause the days of penitence, always taking into account the season of Lent and to substitute abstinence and fast wholly or in part with other forms of penitence and especially works of charity and the exercises of piety. The Constitution went on to say that while "all the faithful are required to do penance by divine law", priests and religious are bound to a more perfect form of fasting beyond the minimum required by canon law, proper to their state in life. "The precept of penitence must be satisfied in a more perfect way by priests...as well as by those who...practice the evangelical counsels."

One full meal during mandatory fast days

Current Canon Law requires that on the days of mandatory fasting, Catholics may eat only one full meal during the day. Additionally, the Church permits a small amount to be taken in the morning and also in the evening. Church requirements on fasting only relate to solid food, not to drink, so any amount of water or other beverages may be consumed.

A Eucharistic fast

A *Eucharistic fast* also existed: until the pontificate of Pope Pius XII abstaining from food and drink from midnight was the condition for receiving Holy Communion.

As Masses after noon and in the evening became common in the West, in 1953, Pope Pius XII modified this to fasting for three hours. The earliest express legislation on the subject is in the Council of Hippo of 393, which allowed an exception on Maundy Thursday. In one of his letters dating from c 400, St Augustine advocates the Eucharistic fast, believing it to be of universal observance and dating back to Apostolic times:

> ...for from that time [of the earliest Church] it
> pleased the Holy Spirit to appoint, for the honour
> of so great a sacrament, that the body of the Lord
> should take the precedence of all other food

entering the mouth of a Christian; and it is for this reason that the custom referred to is universally observed. (*Ep* 54.6)

According to Augustine, this practice made literally true what we believe to be spiritually true. The Eucharist is the first and greatest sustenance for Christians; it is to be preferred above all other means of nourishment, physical and spiritual. Thanks to the Eucharistic fast, the Eucharist was the first food of the day. The practice showed that for the faithful, their "daily bread," the first food that passed their lips each morning, was their first and greatest meal, the very bread of angels.

Throughout the middle Ages until the 20th century, this observance was virtually universal. With the encouragement of more frequent communion and the difficulties occasioned by the Second World War, not to mention evening Masses on days of obligation, dispensations were introduced, which were standardized in Pius XII's Apostolic Constitution *Christus Dominus* (16 January 1953). His *motu proprio Sacram Communionem* of 19 March 1957 laid down that the consumption of water at any time did not break the natural fast; in future a three-hour fast from solid food and alcoholic drink and a one-hour fast from non-alcoholic drink were to be observed before the reception of Holy Communion.

In 1964 Paul VI reduced the period of the Eucharistic fast to one hour before the reception of Holy Communion. Canon law states, "One who is to receive the most Holy Eucharist is to abstain from any food or drink, with the exception only of water and medicine, for at least the period of one hour before Holy Communion" (*CIC* 919 §1). Elderly people, those who are ill, and their carers are excused from the Eucharistic fast (*CIC* 191 §3). Priests and deacons may not dispense one obligated by the Eucharistic fast unless the bishop has expressly granted such power to them (cf. *CIC* 89).

This effort to remain fasting, for a longer or shorter period according to the time when Mass was celebrated, represented a homage paid to the Blessed Sacrament, a sign of the value attached to it and a reminder of its incomparable dignity. Moreover, the fast before receiving Holy Communion creates a physical hunger and thirst for the Lord, which in turn augments the spiritual hunger and thirst we ought to have. Just as in the Old Testament, fasting prepared Moses and Elijah to receive the action of God and to be placed in his presence, so this practice enhances the spiritual disposition we need to receive Christ in the Blessed Sacrament. In a sense, we fast so as not "to spoil our appetite" but to sharpen it for the sharing of the Paschal banquet.

In the Eastern Church

In the *Eastern Church*, days of fasting and abstinence have been numerous; in the Greek Church the total has been as high as 180 in the course of the year. In addition to the 40 days of the great Lent preceding Easter (which at some times and places was a much more extended period), three other Lents are also observed: the Lent of the holy Apostles (June 16-28); Mary's Lent (August 1-14); and the Lent preceding Christmas (November 15-December 24). These three minor Lents did not become obligatory before the 8th century. Wednesday and Friday of every week are observed as days of fasting. During the great Lent, breakfast is in principle prohibited, the fast being therefore total until noon.

Severe abstinence referred to as xerophagy

The law of abstinence is referred to as *xerophagy*, the eating of dry food. In the past, on days of abstinence meat and meat products, including milk, eggs, butter and cheese, as well as fish, oil and wine were forbidden. This traditional custom of severe abstinence is still observed by some of the faithful.

Fasting and the spiritual life

Fasting is the champion of every virtue, the beginning of the struggle, the crown of the abstinent, the beauty of sanctity, the resplendence of chastity, the commencement of the path of Christianity, the mother of prayer, the well-spring of sobriety and prudence, the teacher of stillness, and the precursor of all good works.

(St Isaac the Syrian)

Besides the ordinary effect of fasting in raising the mind, subduing the flesh, confirming goodness, and obtaining a heavenly reward, it is also a great matter to be able to control greediness, and to keep the sensual appetites and the whole body subject to the law of the Spirit; and although we may be able to do but little, the enemy nevertheless stands more in awe of those whom he knows can fast.

(St Francis De Sales)

Fasting and ascesis

Fasting "represents an important ascetical practice, a spiritual arm to do battle against every possible disordered attachment to ourselves. Freely chosen detachment from the pleasure of food and other material goods helps the disciple of Christ to control the appetites of nature, weakened by original sin, whose negative effects impact the entire human person" (Pope Benedict, *Message for Lent* 2009). When we fast we deny our bodily impulses, our spontaneous appetite for food and drink, not because these impulses are in themselves evil, but because they have been disordered by sin and require to be purified through self-discipline. Fasting confronts our tendency to grab and snatch at material things, to see them only as sources of our satisfaction. The world and food are there for us, but limits are set to this order. Not everything is to be enjoyed by consuming it. Fasting signifies a radical change in our relation to God and the world. God, not the self, becomes the centre, and the world is seen as His creation, not something that exists for our own gratification.

Fasting against the "flesh" not the body

Ascetic fasting is directed not against the body but against the "flesh". In the New Testament, flesh is not the same as body. In St Paul's usage, 'flesh' denotes the totality of man, soul and body together, in so far as he is fallen and separated from God; and in the same way 'spirit' denotes the totality of man, soul and body together, in so far as he is redeemed and divinized by grace. Thus the soul as well as the body can become carnal, and the body as well as the soul can become spiritual. When St Paul enumerates the 'works of the flesh' (*Ga* 5:19-21), he includes such things as rivalries, anger and envy, which involve the soul much more than the body. And when he says 'I know that nothing good dwells in my flesh' (*Rm* 7:18), he is speaking of whatever within us is sinful and opposed to God. In making our body spiritual, then, fasting does not suppress the physical aspect of our human nature, but makes our body once more as God intended it to be, a temple of the Holy Spirit.

Our experience of God involves the body

Physical asceticism, which is often viewed in negative terms and associated with disdain for the body, actually tells us that our experience of God involves the body. Without this dimension Christianity is reduced either to an intellectual exercise or to its moral dimension alone. Fasting is part of a true order of things which does not separate body and soul in the spiritual effort. External disciplines impose concrete renunciations to signify and support our movement towards God. Too often today we are content to disdain such practices and to think that our spiritual journey consists in a purely interior progress. A genuine interior life can only grow through the body. As St Paul affirms: 'Your body is a temple of the Holy Spirit. . . Glorify God in your body' (1 *Co* 6:19-20).

The ascetic effort is a liberating agent

So it is right and normal that the body should be part of our spiritual adventure. Our bodies are integral parts of our beings; we need our bodies to express our lives, even the most spiritual part of our lives. But the body as well as the spirit is marked by what Scripture calls sin. The body has to be taken over by grace and transfigured. Although the Christian receives life and grace at baptism, that supernal life does not bring with it the gifts of soul and body that adorned our first parents at creation. Rather the consequences of original sin make human nature a wounded and divided nature. That is why asceticism is necessary, so that we may die to sin and come to the fullness of the resurrection. It is a question of re-establishing order, of transforming our body under the action of the Spirit, to allow the new life received at baptism to develop fully. By contributing to this transfiguration of the entire being into the image of the risen Christ, the ascetic effort is a liberating agent.

An active program towards a goal

Asceticism comes from the Greek *askesis* meaning 'discipline' or 'training' or even 'fighting'. It implies an active programme towards achieving a natural or spiritual goal, or training in order to gain some skill. It means to work at something with great care, artfully; to work something out. It further denotes exertion, diligence, practice, and training. It is important to realize that asceticism has a human value. If we feel that asceticism seems void of religious value it may be because we have forgotten that first of all it is part of human life. Christian asceticism presupposes human asceticism, be it on the part of the athlete, the artist, the soldier: each trains by repeating over and over the same movements or gestures in order to reach a high level of performance. When you choose an end, you also choose the means necessary to reach it, and you exclude whatever is contrary to it. Every specific purpose requires some kind of asceticism.

Realizing in us the beauty of holiness

Christian asceticism should help us become more not less human: an intelligent asceticism can help us in our task of making our life a masterpiece, a work of art. The Greek word askein is also used to designate the work of an artist. The goal of our asceticism is nothing less than to realize in us the beauty of holiness.

Fasting, Prayer and Almsgiving as a triad

In the Sermon on the Mount, Jesus highlights three ways in which people can embody their faith, which are sometimes called "the three eminent good works": prayer, fasting and almsgiving. It is a question of giving our heart in prayer, our material body in fasting, and our material goods in alms. Thus these three great religious acts of the Gospel express, each in its own way, an offering without reserve. In the tradition of the Church fasting is inseparable from prayer and almsgiving, from a living relationship with God and others. St Peter Chrysologus, in one of his sermons, put it this way:

Prayer, almsgiving and fasting are elements of one movement and act, and each gives life to the others. Fasting is the soul of prayer, and almsgiving is the life of fasting. Let no man try to separate them, for they cannot be separated [...]. Prayer and almsgiving and fasting together make up one intercessor for us before God, a single call to the Lord, a trinity of petitions.

This same idea is found in a twentieth century Russian writer, Soloviev, who expressed the union of this triad in this way: prayer unites us to God, almsgiving is an extension of this grace to others, and fasting sanctifies earthly creation through the sanctification of the body.

Self imposed privation becomes a source of charity

Prayer, fasting and almsgiving are also closely united by a relation of cause and effect: fasting demands and makes possible generosity towards others. Thus Isaiah insists that fasts be accompanied by acts of justice and goodness (*Is* 58:3-10). But in Christian practice the relation is even stricter; what one deprives oneself of in fasting is given to others. The second-century Shepherd of Hermas lays down this rule which has a modern ring: on fast days let the Christian be content with bread and water, calculating the money thus saved and giving it as a gift to the poor. But almsgiving means more than this. It is to give not only our money but our time, not only what we have but what we are; it is to give a part of ourselves. Self-imposed privation thus becomes a source of charity. In his "instruments of good works," St Benedict's maxim "to love fasting" is followed by "to relieve the poor."

Physical fasting is meaningless
without spiritual prayer

Fasting as a physical effort is totally meaningless without its spiritual counterpart, *prayer*. Prayer and fasting are mentioned together in many passages of Scripture, for "prayer is good when accompanied by fasting" (*Tb* 12:8). Anna worshipped God "with prayer and fasting night and day" (*Lk* 2:37), as did St Paul and the early Christian community. Fasting "transmits prayer to heaven; like a wing it causes it to ascend" (St Basil). Without the corresponding spiritual effort of prayer, without feeding ourselves with divine reality, without discovering our dependence on God in prayer, physical fasting would be meaningless. Fasting for God's sake means asking God for help when we feel weak, making it God-centred. Often we consider fasting as a sacrifice added to prayer, but in fact, some sort of bodily abstinence is the necessary preparation for one's real prayer. Fasting intensifies our prayer to God, as St John Vianney recognized: when a priest complained to him about his parishioners, the saint asked, "Have you fasted for them?"

Spiritual Fasting

Fasting is not a mere matter of diet. It is moral as well as physical. True fasting is to be converted in heart and will; it is to return to God, to come home like the Prodigal to our Father's house. In the words of St John Chrysostom, it means "abstinence not only from food but from sins." The fast, he insists, "should be kept not by the mouth alone but also by the eye, the ear, the feet, the hands and all the members of the body: the eye must abstain from impure sights, the ear from malicious gossip, the hands from acts of injustice." It is useless to fast from food, protests St Basil, and yet to indulge in cruel criticism and slander: "you do not eat meat, but you devour your brother." Since food restriction aims at interior purification, restraint and moderation with regard to food and drink must always suggest a more interior discipline, such as fasting from bad thoughts, talking, etc.

The rich texts of the Lenten liturgy are full of this theme. In most of the prayers at Mass at this season you find expressions like these: "The abstinence which we observe in the body may we also practice with a sincere heart" (Fri. after Ash Wed); "May our minds shine forth with longing for you as we subject ourselves to frugality in the things of the body" (Tues. 1st week); "As we put a curb on longing for things of earth, may we learn to love the things of heaven (post-communion); "May your family, O Lord, while fasting from food, pursue holiness by abstaining from sin" (Mon. 2nd week); "By the Lenten fast may we so purify ourselves that we may be able to celebrate the solemnity of the Paschal sacrifice with a pure and sincere heart" (Fri. 2nd week). "As we deprive ourselves of bodily food, so also may we fast from sin in our mind" (Fri. 3rd week); "Restrain our senses from all harmful excess" (Mon. 3rd week).

Thus the fasting and abstinence of Lent must always be the basis for growing in interior purity and so prepare us to receive Easter not as mere permission to eat and drink but indeed as the end of the old in us, as our entrance into the new life of the risen Christ, the reception of a new heart. That which is exterior is ordained to that which is interior; and we use material things to help us attain to spiritual realities. If this were not so, bodily penances would be useless, even occasions of pride and a false sense of security.

Fasting and the New Creation

Fasting not only prepares us for prayer, it is also the manifestation of prayer; it is, as it were, the prayer of the body: "By its beauty, fasting etches the image of eternal life into the body; the practice suggests the condition of the new age; it teaches us what spiritual food we shall receive at the resurrection" (Martyrius Sahdônâ, seventh century Syrian bishop). Fasting points to the new creation of resurrection; it prepares the body for resurrection, opening it to grace.

From this perspective the Christian's asceticism is not only a means, but a sign of his liberty in relation to his earthly life; it signifies his membership of heaven. If the Christian fasts it is because man does not live by bread alone; if he abstains from drink it is because he knows there is living water. He points to the fact that in the age to come our principle of life will be the spirit of Christ. Christ is our nourishment, our drink, our life-breath. So our asceticism is not only about purification, reparation, conversion; it points to our status as citizens of heaven. By his fasts, the believer tells God that he desires the eternal blessings that are to come rather than the finite blessings of this life.

The fasting is ultimately for the feasting

Fasting means rediscovering our body as a temple of God's presence; recovering a religious respect for the body, for food, for the rhythm of life. One learns to receive food and everything else as real gifts of God. Fasting from the food and drink of this present world is for Christians a sign of our expectation of the feasting in the new world, the world of the resurrection, on the food and drink of everlasting life. Our fasting orients us towards Christ's second coming, just as the Eucharistic fast orients us towards receiving him at Mass. The fasting is ultimately for the feasting.

The Friday penance – rediscovering Catholic identity

The Bishops' decision to re-introduce the obligatory practice of abstaining from meat on Friday as a weekly ascetical discipline is the recognition that Catholics need to recover outward signs of their collective identity. The Friday abstinence was a universal act that reminded Catholics that they were called to live differently from non-Catholics around them and it was recognised by non Catholics as something that Catholics did.

This was one of the reasons invoked by the Bishops of England and Wales when they announced, in May 2011, the re-introduction of abstinence from meat on Friday as an obligatory penitential act for Catholics. The Bishops' resolution states:

> "Every Friday is set aside by the Church as a special day of penance, for it is the day of the death of our Lord. The law of the Church requires Catholics to

abstain from meat on Fridays, or some other form of food, or to observe some other form of penance laid down by the Bishops' Conference. The Bishops wish to re-establish the practice of Friday penance in the lives of the faithful as a clear and distinctive mark of their own Catholic identity. It is important that all the faithful be united in a common celebration of Friday penance. Respectful of this, and in accordance with the mind of the whole Church, the Bishops' Conference wishes to remind all Catholics in England and Wales of the obligation of Friday Penance. The Bishops have decided to re-establish the practice that this should be fulfilled by abstaining from meat. Many may wish to go beyond this simple act of common witness and mark each Friday with a time of prayer and further self-sacrifice."

The Bishops' statement concluded. "In all these ways we unite our sacrifices to the sacrifice of Christ, who gave up his very life for our salvation." The Bishops said those who do not eat meat normally should abstain from some other food on Fridays. The discipline re-commenced on September 16th 2011, the first anniversary of Pope Benedict's state visit to the UK.

Religion is not a purely private affair. Commenting on the resolution, Archbishop Nichols stressed that the bishops "recognise that the best habits are those which are acquired as part of a common resolve and common witness...It is important that all the faithful be united in a common celebration of Friday penance."

Back in the tenth century, Pope St Leo the Great underlined the special meaning and power of public fasting of the whole Church, when it takes on an external, universal, obligatory character:

"The exercise of self-restraint, which some decide for themselves by their own judgment, pertains to the benefit of certain individuals; but a fast undertaken by the whole Church leaves no one out from the general purification. It is then that the people of God become powerful, when the hearts of all the faithful come together in the unity of holy obedience, because in the camp of the Christian fighters, there is a similar preparation all round, and the fortification is the same everywhere. Although the watchful fury of the cruel enemy rages and spreads out hidden snares everywhere, he can take no one, he can wound no one, if he finds everyone armed, everyone active, everyone sharing in the works of mercy."

Wouldn't it be more sacrificial for someone to give up foods that they really loved such as chocolate rather than meat which one may not care for that much? And other works and means of doing penance: prayer, acts of self-denial, almsgiving and works of personal charity, attending Mass daily or several times a week, praying the rosary, making the way of the cross, visiting the sick—all of these can be more meaningful and demanding than simply abstaining from meat on Friday.

Certainly almsgiving, love for others expressed in practical form, works of compassion and forgiveness have always accompanied fasting, but were not, until recently, considered as a *substitute* for it. However valuable and good these compensations may be, the asceticism of fasting and other bodily practices remain irreplaceable, being of another order. On the one hand, fasting and abstinence is something we do in common with everyone else in the Church; there is a strength that comes with following the accepted patterns of the Church's traditions, when, in the words of the Bishop's resolution, *all the faithful [are] united in a common celebration of Friday penance.* On the other hand, the purpose of fasting is not to "give up" things.

Fasting, as we have seen, is a much broader reality than giving up chocolate. While fasting takes the form of refraining from eating, it is primarily designed to submit the body to a spiritual discipline and thereby "sealing" our entire being so that we can concentrate on higher things. In this case it takes in the whole person, not just this or that activity. There is also a sense that the desires we find within us can be summed up in our desire for food, that our appetite for food and drink contains all other appetites. During the fast we deny our bodily impulses—for example, our spontaneous appetite for food and drink—not because these impulses are in themselves evil, but because they have been disordered by sin and require to be purified through self-discipline.

Pope Benedict expressed it in this way: fasting is "a spiritual arm to do battle against every possible disordered attachment to ourselves." He further commented that fasting is a "therapy to heal all that prevents [us] from conformity to the will of God", and "assists us to mortify our egoism and open our heart to love of God and neighbour." The main purpose of fasting is to gain mastery over oneself and to conquer the passions of the flesh, so that we are no longer ruled by the selfish desire to grasp and to exploit. It is to liberate oneself from dependence on the things of this world in order to concentrate on the things of the Kingdom of God. Fasting always points to other nourishment, to the bread that does not perish.

Fasting is in part about training ourselves to distinguish our needs from wants, to discover what our real needs are. We all need to develop the habit of saying *no* to ourselves, and this is acquired only through regular spiritual exercise—namely through fasting. From this point of view sin appears as selfishness, exploitation, the desire to make use of and consume the world instead of seeing it as God's gift. Fasting puts between us and the world a distance full of wonder, respect and thanksgiving. Fasting can lead to a transformation whereby our dependence on food and matter is not total, not absolute; united to prayer, grace and thanksgiving these things can become spiritual. The quality of our life is, in other words, not based on our power of consuming or buying or with quick fixes and instant satisfactions. Deeply understood, fasting becomes the means by which man recovers his true spiritual nature and freedom, a freedom regained with regard to those passions which turn us away from Christ.

If the importance of fasting has diminished today, could part of the problem be that fasting is seen only as a penance?

Yes. To be sure, as St Paul reminds us, "Continually we carry about in our bodies the death of Jesus, so that in our bodies the life of Jesus may be revealed" (2 *Co* 4:10). We are exhorted to convert our whole lives—body and soul—to the Lord. This conversion process involves doing penance—including bodily mortification like fasting—for our sins and weaknesses, which in turn strengthens and heals us. But St Thomas Aquinas reminds us that the purpose of fasting is twofold: it is useful not only for prevention and atonement of sin, but also for lifting up the mind to things of the Spirit.

An earlier tradition can help us here. Citing St Basil, Pope Benedict reminded us in his Lenten address in 2009 that fasting was ordained in Paradise. Fasting, as the Fathers of the Church noted, existed before the "original sin" of Adam and Eve, and it was not ordered as a cure for their sin. The fasting in Paradise consisted of abstaining of certain food—namely of "the fruit of the tree." God's commandment to Adam and Even not to eat of the particular fruit was issued as a method of man's discipline of self-control and spiritual growth, as they were not yet in their final state.

But it is also important to note the true meaning of the word penance. Too often it is understood only as voluntary affliction, aimed at reparation for sin. But in fact the biblical notion is much wider and more profound. The Latin *poenitentia* translates the Greek *metanoia*, and this means a turning, a change in the direction of things. Metanoia is not just regret for the past nor even sorrow for sin, but a fundamental transformation of our outlook, a new way of looking at ourselves, at others, at God. Repentance is not about guilt or remorse or self-pity, but conversion, the re-centering of our life upon the one thing necessary; it refers to a complete change of direction, a change of mind which is a question of a lasting state and not of a punishment one inflicts on oneself in passing. If true penance means being converted, it must result in a permanent mode of life. A change of mind, evangelical *metanoia* means necessarily a change of habits, a new manner of living which includes the body itself. Fasting is at the service of such a conversion: it trains us to be content with what is necessary, by freeing us from artificial needs created by our consumeristic society; it helps us to see that the quality of our life is not based on our power of consuming or buying or with quick fixes and instant satisfactions.

Fasting is not an act of mortification for mortification's sake. On the contrary, fasting for a Christian should be a joyful experience, because it is a self-discipline which we voluntarily impose upon ourselves in the ongoing effort to simplify our lives, to reconquer interior unity, order and freedom, to struggle to overcome our sins and to grow in love and communion with God and others.

The value and meaning of fasting

Benedict XVI on Lent

He fasted for forty days and forty nights, and afterwards he was hungry (*Mt* 4, 1-2)

At the beginning of Lent, which constitutes an itinerary of more intense spiritual training, the Liturgy sets before us again three penitential practices that are very dear to the biblical and Christian tradition—prayer, almsgiving, fasting—to prepare us to better celebrate Easter and thus experience God's power that, as we shall hear in the Paschal Vigil, "dispels all evil, washes guilt away, restores lost innocence, brings mourners joy, casts out hatred, brings us peace and humbles earthly pride" (*Paschal Præconium*).

I wish to focus my reflections especially on the value and meaning of fasting. Indeed, Lent recalls the forty days of our Lord's fasting in the desert, which He undertook before entering into His public ministry. We read in the Gospel: "Jesus was led up by the Spirit into the wilderness to be tempted by the devil. He fasted for forty days and forty nights, and afterwards He was hungry" (*Mt* 4, 1-2). Like Moses, who fasted before receiving the tablets of the Law (cf. *Ex* 34, 28) and Elijah's fast before meeting the Lord on Mount Horeb (cf. 1 *K* 19, 8), Jesus, too, through prayer and fasting, prepared Himself for the mission that lay before Him, marked at the start by a serious battle with the tempter.

An instrument to restore friendship with God

We might wonder what value and meaning there is for us Christians in depriving ourselves of something that in itself is good and useful for our bodily sustenance. The Sacred Scriptures and the entire Christian tradition teach that fasting is a great help to avoid sin and all that leads to it. For this reason, the history of salvation is replete with occasions that invite fasting. In the very first pages of Sacred Scripture, the Lord commands man to abstain from partaking of the prohibited fruit: "You may freely eat of every tree of the garden; but of the tree of the knowledge of good and evil you shall not eat, for in the day that you eat of it you shall die" (*Gn* 2, 16-17). Commenting on the divine injunction, Saint Basil observes that "fasting was ordained in Paradise," and "the first commandment in this sense was delivered to Adam."

He thus concludes: "'You shall not eat' is a law of fasting and abstinence" (cf. *Sermo de jejunio*: PG 31, 163, 98). Since all of us are weighed down by sin and its consequences, fasting is proposed to us as an instrument to restore friendship with God.

Such was the case with Ezra, who, in preparation for the journey from exile back to the Promised Land, calls upon the assembled people to fast so that "we might humble ourselves before our God" (8, 21). The Almighty heard their prayer and assured them of His favor and protection. In the same way, the people of Nineveh, responding to Jonah's call to repentance, proclaimed a fast, as a sign of their sincerity, saying: "Who knows, God may yet repent and turn from his fierce anger, so that we perish not?" (3, 9). In this instance, too, God saw their works and spared them.

True fasting is to do the will of the Heavenly Father

In the New Testament, Jesus brings to light the profound motive for fasting, condemning the attitude of the Pharisees, who scrupulously observed the prescriptions of the law, but whose hearts were far from God. True fasting, as the divine Master repeats elsewhere, is rather to do the will of the Heavenly Father, who "sees in secret, and will reward you" (*Mt* 6, 18). He Himself sets the example, answering Satan, at the end of the forty days spent in the desert that "man shall not live by bread alone, but by every word that proceeds from the mouth of God" (*Mt* 4, 4). The true fast is thus directed to eating the "true food," which is to do the Father's will (cf. *Jn* 4, 34). If, therefore, Adam disobeyed the Lord's command "of the tree of the knowledge of good and evil you shall not eat," the believer, through fasting, intends to submit himself humbly to God, trusting in His goodness and mercy.

If you pray, fast; if you fast, show mercy

The practice of fasting is very present in the first Christian community (cf. *Ac* 13, 3; 14, 22; 27, 21; 2 Co 6, 5). The Church Fathers, too, speak of the force of fasting to bridle sin, especially the lusts of the "old Adam," and open in the heart of the believer a path to God. Moreover, fasting is a practice that is encountered frequently and recommended by the saints of every age. Saint Peter Chrysologus writes: "Fasting is the soul of prayer, mercy is the lifeblood of fasting. So if you pray, fast; if you fast, show mercy; if you want your petition to be heard, hear the petition of others. If you do not close your ear to others, you open God's ear to yourself" (*Sermo* 43: PL 52, 320. 322).

A therapy to heal

In our own day, fasting seems to have lost something of its spiritual meaning, and has taken on, in a culture characterized by the search for material well-being, a therapeutic value for the care of one's body. Fasting certainly brings benefits to physical well-being, but for believers, it is, in the first place, a "therapy" to heal all that prevents them from conformity to the will of God. In the Apostolic Constitution *Pænitemini* of 1966, the Servant of God Paul VI saw the need to present fasting within the call of every Christian to "no longer live for himself, but for Him who loves him and gave himself for him ... he will also have to live for his brethren" (cf. Ch. I). Lent could be a propitious time to present again the norms contained in the Apostolic Constitution, so that the authentic and perennial significance of this long held practice may be rediscovered, and thus assist us to mortify our egoism and open our heart to love of God and neighbour, the first and greatest Commandment of the new Law and compendium of the entire Gospel (cf. *Mt* 22, 34-40).

The hunger and thirst for God

The faithful practice of fasting contributes, moreover, to conferring unity to the whole person, body and soul, helping to avoid sin and grow in intimacy with the

Lord. Saint Augustine, who knew all too well his own negative impulses, defining them as "twisted and tangled knottiness" (*Confessions*, II, 10.18), writes: "I will certainly impose privation, but it is so that He will forgive me, to be pleasing in His eyes, that I may enjoy His delightfulness" (*Sermo* 400, 3, 3: PL 40, 708). Denying material food, which nourishes our body, nurtures an interior disposition to listen to Christ and be fed by His saving word. Through fasting and praying, we allow Him to come and satisfy the deepest hunger that we experience in the depths of our being: the hunger and thirst for God.

Open your eyes to charity

At the same time, fasting is an aid to open our eyes to the situation in which so many of our brothers and sisters live. In his *First Letter*, Saint John admonishes: "If anyone has the world's goods, and sees his brother in need, yet shuts up his bowels of compassion from him—how does the love of God abide in him?" (3, 17). Voluntary fasting enables us to grow in the spirit of the Good Samaritan, who bends low and goes to the help of his suffering brother (cf. Encyclical *Deus caritas est*, 15). By freely embracing an act of self-denial for the sake of another, we make a statement that our brother or sister in need is not a stranger. It is precisely to keep alive this welcoming and attentive attitude towards our brothers and sisters that I encourage the parishes and every other community to intensify in Lent the custom of private and communal fasts, joined to the reading of the Word of God, prayer and almsgiving. From the beginning, this has been the hallmark of the Christian community, in which special collections were taken up (cf. 2 *Co* 8-9; *Rm* 15, 25-27), the faithful being invited to give to the poor what had been set aside from their fast (*Didascalia* Ap., V, 20, 18). This practice needs to be rediscovered and encouraged again in our day, especially during the liturgical season of Lent.

The custody of our senses

From what I have said thus far, it seems abundantly clear that fasting represents an important ascetical practice, a spiritual arm to do battle against every possible disordered attachment to ourselves. Freely chosen detachment from the pleasure of food and other material goods helps the disciple of Christ to control the appetites of nature, weakened by original sin, whose negative effects impact the entire human person. Quite opportunely, an ancient hymn of the Lenten liturgy exhorts: "*Utamur ergo parcius, / verbis cibis et potibus, / somno, iocis et arctius / perstemus in custodia* – Let us use sparingly words, food and drink, sleep and amusements. May we be more alert in the custody of our senses."

The complete gift of self to God

It is good to see how the ultimate goal of fasting is to help each one of us, as the Servant of God Pope John Paul II wrote, to make the complete gift of self to God (cf. Encyclical *Veritatis splendor*, 21). May every family and Christian community use well this time of Lent, therefore, in order to cast aside all that distracts the spirit and grow in whatever nourishes the soul, moving it to love of God and neighbour. I am thinking especially of a greater commitment to prayer, *lectio divina*, recourse to the Sacrament of Reconciliation and active participation in the Eucharist, especially the Holy Sunday Mass. With this interior disposition, let us enter the penitential spirit of Lent. May the Blessed Virgin Mary, *Causa nostrae laetitiae*, accompany and support us in the effort to free our heart from slavery to sin, making it ever more a living tabernacle of God.

(*Message of His Holiness Benedict XVI for Lent 2009*)

Questions and answers

Some people say that God's people need not fast since we are saved by grace and not by works, and that this practice cramps the liberty of the Christian by adding other observances and rules.

St Thomas Aquinas asks this same question. He answers: "The fasting regulations in force, by Episcopal authority and custom, do not infringe the liberty of the faithful but serve rather to break the bondage of sin, of which St Paul writes: "You, brethren, have been called unto liberty; only make not liberty an occasion to the flesh. (*Ga* 5:13)." Fasting, like all other ascetical practices, aims at the liberation of man.

Our ascetic discipline is meant to help us develop habits of sacrifice and self-discipline so as to overcome those obstacles to real change in ourselves, to become capable of the greatest love of all. Asceticism should have the effect of liberating us from self-love and egoism and transforming us from individuals into persons capable of communion, love and the free gift of ourselves. "This is why we take on solitude, fasting, vigils, work, nakedness," writes St John Cassian. "For this we practise the reading of the Scripture, together with all other virtuous activities, and we do so to hold our hearts free of the harm of every dangerous passion and in order to rise step by step to the high point of love" (*Conf* 1:7). We perform these ascetical practices, says Cassian, "to hold our hearts free...and to rise to love." Freedom is the first result of asceticism, then love; because the gift of self that is love requires the freedom to give ourselves. But the struggle involves the whole person, including the body. It is not just a matter of intention and desire.

Asceticism takes seriously the fact that we cannot serve two masters, and that the alternative to obeying God is serving idols. It tells us that we need to educate our inner life, refine and purify our love; the effort and struggle of our ascetic effort is meant to open us to the gift of God, to help prepare our entire being, body and soul, to receive the gifts of His grace. Such asceticism is at the service of Christian revelation which affirms that our true freedom is revealed when we are open to the gift of God and capable of giving ourselves for love of God and others.

Christian asceticism is dedicated to forming us in true freedom: not by removing restrictions external to ourselves, but by choosing God to be our master, loosening the shackles of other masters to be able to embrace God and His commandments, and then to live freely by the norm we have chosen. Again this is not just a matter of intention or desire, nor is choosing God a once and for all choice. The other masters do not give up their hold easily, and we do not easily let them go. "We must be afraid of drunkenness and gluttony, not of fasting," exhorted St John Chrysostom in one of his homilies. "For they bind our hands behind our backs and surrender us as slaves and captives to the tyranny of the passions, which resemble a most dangerous mistress. Fasting, however, who finds us as slaves and prisoners, loosens the bonds and delivers us from the tyranny, she restores us to our former freedom."

More recently, Pope Paul VI used the same language in his apostolic constitution *Pænitemini* (1966), "Mortification aims at the liberation of man, who often finds himself, because of concupiscence, almost chained by his own senses. Through 'corporal fasting' man regains strength, and the wound inflicted on the dignity of our nature by intemperance is cured by the medicine of a salutary abstinence."

The rules of the Church help us in all this, like sticks placed in the ground to support the growth of plants. The Church, says St Thomas Aquinas, in her wisdom provides for the weakness of human nature by positive legislation concerning fasting, just as secular authority has the right of making more definite regulations than the precepts of natural law to promote the welfare of their citizens. The natural law requires us to pay just debts; the secular authority may order them to be paid within a certain time and with certain formalities.

The Church, he says, may surely take similar means to secure the well-being of its members.

Isn't fasting too much for our contemporary world? Is it true that modern man is weaker than his forebears?

Perhaps it is truer to say that if corporal ascesis no longer has a place in modern life, it is because we no longer feel it is important. When we feel a need, we find the strength to act and organize our life accordingly. We do have as much strength and energy as our forebears, but we employ them differently. The training of athletes demands restrictions and self-denials of every kind. Many of our contemporaries are willing to fast for reasons of health or beauty, in order to lose weight; Christians are invited to do as much for the sake of the heavenly Kingdom, in imitation of Christ.

As traditionally practiced in the Church, fasting has always been difficult and has always involved some hardship. Once St Seraphim of Sarov was asked why the miracles of grace, so abundantly manifest in the past, were no longer apparent in his own day, and to this he replied: "Only one thing is lacking—a firm resolve."

Moreover, one of the aims of fasting is to make us conscious of our dependence upon God. If abstinence from food involves a considerable measure of real hunger, and also a feeling of tiredness, the purpose of this is to bring us to appreciate that word of Christ: "Without Me you can do nothing" (*Jn* 15:5). If we always take our fill of food and drink, we easily grow over-confident in our own abilities and develop a false sense of autonomy and self-sufficiency. The observance of a physical fast undermines this self-complacency, and shows that it is only in our Lord and with Him that our ascent to Him is accomplished. The aim of all asceticism is to practise humility, contrition of heart, to develop a gentle disposition, to recognize that God brings us to divine perfection. This is not to deny our human effort, but in order to divinize our efforts, make them transparent to divine action; we have to refrain from putting excessive confidence in ourselves.

A story from the desert fathers expresses this well. Some monks ask Abba Moses: What is the value of our fasts and vigils? Abba Moses replies. "The aim of fasts and vigils is so that a monk may give up on himself that he may be led into humility." In other words he is to feel the extent of his own helplessness, in order to say, this is really beyond me, I need God. The saying goes on: "When he bears this fruit, a monk touches the heart of God, and God comes to the rescue with a miracle." The power of God is now able to step forth and renew the whole man. From the cross we pass to the resurrection. The Lord always gives us the grace to bear things, to do what is necessary. Indeed He is carrying the weight in us.

We saw that ascesis means training, exercise, training oneself. But this is not to say that it is an exercise of one's possibilities, a test of one's own strength. Ascesis is rather an exercise in grace and because grace is always rooted in weakness, this ascesis is an acting out of the mystery of weakness and grace. God does not give Himself according to the measure of our efforts. He seeks our weakness so that His strength and grace may grow in us without limit (2 Co 12:9). Here too the paschal mystery gives ascesis deeper meaning and significance, and shows it to be a mystery of weakness and grace. It is in our weakness and emptiness that the power of Christ is most active and manifest.

As those who have practised it know, true fasting will lead to temptation, weakness, and irritation. The prayers in the liturgy of Lent are also full of this theme, asking help in our weakness. In other words, it can be a real fight, and we shall probably fail many times. But the very discovery of Christian life as struggle and effort is an essential aspect of fasting. When we're fighting, at least we're alive. And just as we cannot pray without actually giving time to prayer, so too we cannot learn to fast properly without some actual abstaining from food. But if, having failed and surrendered to our appetites, we start again and do not give up no matter how many times we fail, sooner or later our fasting, and indeed all our ascetical efforts, will bear spiritual fruit. There are no short cuts to holiness.

Yet it would be misleading to speak only of this element of weariness and hunger. Fasting also brings a sense of lightness, alertness, freedom and joy. Even if the fast proves difficult at first, afterwards it can help us to think more clearly, and to work more decisively. As many doctors acknowledge, periodical fasts contribute to bodily hygiene. While involving genuine self-denial, fasting does not seek to do violence to our body but rather to restore it to health and balance. Most of us in the Western world habitually eat more than we need. Fasting liberates our body and makes it a partner in the work of prayer, alert and responsive to the voice of the Spirit.

How should one fast?

The Catholic Church makes a distinction between the two terms: abstinence and fasting. Abstinence concerns the types of food eaten, irrespective of quantity: Until the fourteenth century, most Western Christians, in common with their brethren in the Orthodox East, abstained during Lent not only from meat but from animal products, such as eggs, milk, butter and cheese. Today, abstinence forbids the use of meat, but not of eggs, milk products or condiments made of animal fat. Fasting signifies a limitation on the number of meals or on the amount of food that can be taken.

To sum up the requirements: Catholics between the ages of 18 and 59 are obliged to fast on Ash Wednesday and Good Friday. In addition, all Catholics 14 years old and older must abstain from meat on Ash Wednesday, Good Friday and all the Fridays of Lent, as well as on all Fridays throughout the year. Fasting means partaking of only one full meal a day. Some food (not equaling another full meal) is permitted at breakfast and around midday or in the evening—depending on when a person chooses to eat the main or full meal. This is a mild form of fasting, but one which leaves the person always a little on the hungry side and aware that he is depriving himself of his regular fare.

As circumstances vary, it is up to each one to decide which level is "appropriate" since this is a matter best worked out in each Christian's own setting. When fasting, we should eat simply and modestly. The Fathers simply state, as a guiding principle, that we should never eat to satiety but always rise from the table feeling that we could have taken more.

If you are new to fasting, you may find the onset of hunger pangs uncomfortable. But they are not harmful; they are simply part of the fast. The first few days of a long fasting period are often the most difficult. Do not be discouraged by headaches, fatigue, etc. at the beginning of a fast—they will disappear or reduce in intensity. Often moderate exercise, like a short walk, can make a surprising difference in your energy levels.

Ultimately to fast means not a mere change of diet, what is forbidden and what permitted; it means to be hungry, or in a state of half-hunger, and yet to discover that, as Our Lord taught us, man does not live by bread alone.

The points given here are of course only one part, the most external part, of a true fast, which will include increased prayer and other spiritual disciplines, and may include resolutions to set aside other aspects of our day-to-day life (such as caffeine or television), or to take up practices such as visiting the sick.

Endnotes

[1] The words *and fasting* are found in the great majority of manuscripts, but the Jerusalem Bible translation and some other versions omit the reference on the grounds that it was not included in some of the early texts.

[2] As Jesus' answer suggests, the challenge to turn stones into bread is a reference to the episode of the manna in *Ex* 16. The temptation here is to doubt God's power to provide, to be anxious about the morrow. The next temptation seeks to challenge God by means of a miracle as in the episode of Manassah (*Ex* 17:1-7; *Nm* 20:13: "Is the Lord in the midst of us or not?") But Our Lord refuses to satisfy our desire for the marvellous. The third temptation to adore the devil in return for power recalls the episode of the golden calf.

[3] Basil seems to have been the first Greek theologian to have put forward this particular explanation of original sin: that the first sin of Adam and Eve was ravenous greed!